CATCHING THE BIG FISH

CATCHING THE BIG FISH

MEDITATION, CONSCIOUSNESS, AND CREATIVITY

DAVID LYNCH

A TARCHERPERIGEE BOOK

tarcherperigee
An imprint of Penguin Random House LLC
375 Hudson Street
New York, New York 10014

First trade paperback edition 2007

First hardcover edition 2006; first paperback edition 2007; edition with new afterword 2016

Most TarcherPerigee books are available at special quantity discounts for bulk purchase for sales promotions, premiums, fund-raising, and educational needs. Special books or book excerpts also can be created to fit specific needs. For details, write: SpecialMarkets@penguinrandomhouse.com.

The Library of Congress has cataloged the hardcover edition as follows:

Lynch, David, date.
Catching the big fish : meditation, consciousness, and creativity / David Lynch.
p.   cm.
ISBN 9781585425402 (hc.)
ISBN 9781585426126 (pbk.)
ISBN 9780143130147 (10th Anniversary ed.)
1.Transcendental Meditation.   2. Creative ability—Religious aspects.   3. Creation
(Literary, artistic, etc.)   I.Title.
BF637.T68L96   2007   2006037103
158.1'25—dc22

Printed in the United States of America
11th Printing

BOOK DESIGN BY CLAIRE VACCARO

To His Holiness Maharishi Mahesh Yogi

CONTENTS

INTRODUCTION

Ideas are like fish.

If you want to catch little fish, you can stay in the shallow water. But if you want to catch the big fish, you've got to go deeper.

Down deep, the fish are more powerful and more pure. They're huge and abstract. And they're very beautiful.

I look for a certain kind of fish that is important to me, one that can translate to cinema. But there are all kinds of fish swimming down there. There are fish for business, fish for sports. There are fish for everything.

Everything, anything that is a thing, comes up from the deepest level. Modern physics calls that level the Unified Field. The more your consciousness—your awareness—is expanded, the deeper you go toward this source, and the bigger the fish you can catch.

My thirty-three-year practice of the Transcendental Meditation program has been central to my work in film and painting and to all areas of my life. For me it has been the way to dive deeper in search of the big fish. In this book, I want to share some of those experiences with you.

THE FIRST DIVE

He whose happiness is within, whose contentment is within,
whose light is all within, that yogi, being one
with Brahman, attains eternal freedom in divine consciousness.

BHAGAVAD-GITA

When I first heard about meditation, I had zero interest in it. I wasn't even curious. It sounded like a waste of time.

What got me interested, though, was the phrase "true happiness lies within." At first I thought it sounded kind of mean, because it doesn't tell you where the "within" is, or how to get there. But still it had a ring of truth. And I began to think that maybe meditation was a way to go within.

I looked into meditation, asked some questions, and started contemplating different forms. At that moment, my sister called and said she had been doing Transcendental Meditation for six months. There was something in her voice. A change. A quality of happiness. And I thought, *That's what I want.*

So in July 1973 I went to the TM center in Los Angeles and met an instructor, and I liked her. She looked like Doris Day. And she taught me this technique. She gave me a mantra, which is a sound-vibration-thought. You don't meditate on the meaning of it, but it's a very specific sound-vibration-thought.

She took me into a little room to have my first meditation. I sat down, closed my eyes, started this mantra, and it was as if I were in an elevator and the cable had been cut. Boom! I fell into bliss—pure bliss. And I was just *in* there. Then the teacher said, "It's time to come out; it's been twenty minutes." And I said, "IT'S ALREADY BEEN TWENTY MINUTES?!" And she said, "Shhhh!" because other people were meditating. It seemed so familiar, but also so new and powerful. After that, I said the word "unique" should be reserved for this experience.

It takes you to an ocean of pure consciousness, pure knowingness. But it's familiar; it's *you*. And right away a sense of happiness emerges—not a goofball happiness, but a thick beauty.

I have never missed a meditation in thirty-three years. I meditate once in the morning and again in the afternoon, for about twenty minutes each time. Then I go about the business of my day. And I find that the joy of doing increases. Intuition increases. The pleasure of life grows. And negativity recedes.

*It would be easier to roll up the entire sky into
a small cloth than it would be to obtain true happiness
without knowing the Self.*

UPANISHADS

When I started meditating, I was filled with anxieties and fears. I felt a sense of depression and anger.

I often took out this anger on my first wife. After I had been meditating for about two weeks, she came to me and said, "What's going on?" I was quiet for a moment. But finally I said, "What do you mean?" And she said, "This anger, where did it go?" And I hadn't even realized that it had lifted.

I call that depression and anger the Suffocating Rubber Clown Suit of Negativity. It's *suffocating*, and that rubber *stinks*. But once you start meditating and diving within, the clown suit starts to dissolve. You finally realize how putrid was the stink when it starts to go. Then, when it dissolves, you have freedom.

Anger and depression and sorrow are beautiful things in a story, but they're like poison to the filmmaker or artist. They're like a vise grip on creativity. If you're in that grip, you can hardly get out of bed, much less experience the flow of creativity and ideas. You must have clarity to create. You have to be able to catch ideas.

I started out just as a regular person, growing up in the Northwest. My father was a research scientist for the Department of Agriculture, studying trees. So I was in the woods a lot. And the woods for a child are magical. I lived in what people call small towns. My world was what would be considered about a city block, maybe two blocks. Everything occurred in that space. All the dreaming, all my friends existed in that small world. But to me it seemed so huge and magical. There was plenty of time available to dream and be with friends.

I liked to paint and I liked to draw. And I often thought, wrongly, that when you got to be an adult, you stopped painting and drawing and did something more serious. In the ninth grade, my family moved to Alexandria, Virginia. On the front lawn of my girlfriend's house one night, I met a guy named Toby Keeler. As we were talking, he said his father was a painter. I thought maybe he might have been a house painter, but further talking got me around to the fact that he was a fine artist.

This conversation changed my life. I had been somewhat interested in science, but I suddenly knew that I wanted to be a painter. And I wanted to live the art life.

In high school, I read Robert Henri's book *The Art Spirit*, which prompted the idea of the art life. For me, living the art life meant a dedication to painting—a complete dedication to it, making everything else secondary.

That, I thought, is the only way you're going to get in deep and discover things. So anything that distracts from that path of discovery is not part of the art life, in that way of thinking. Really, the art life means a freedom. And it seems, I think, a hair selfish. But it doesn't have to be selfish; it just means that you need time.

Bushnell Keeler, the father of my friend Toby, always had this expression: "If you want to get one hour of good painting in, you have to have four hours of uninterrupted time."

And that's basically true. You don't just start painting. You have to sit for a while and get some kind of mental idea in order to go and make the right moves. And you need a whole bunch of materials at the ready. For example, you need to build frame-work stretchers for the canvas. It can take a long time just to prepare something to paint on. And then you go to work. The idea just needs to be enough to get you started, because, for me, whatever follows is a process of action and reaction. It's always a process of building and then destroying. And then, out of this destruction, discovering a thing and building on it. Nature plays a huge part in it. Putting difficult materials together—like baking something in sunlight, or using one material that fights another material—causes its own organic reaction. Then it's a matter of sitting back and studying it and studying it and studying it; and suddenly, you find you're leaping up out of your chair and going in and doing the next thing. That's action and reaction.

But if you know that you've got to be somewhere in half an hour, there's no way you can achieve that. So the art life means a freedom to have time for the good things to happen. There's not always a lot of time for other things.

So I was a painter. I painted and I went to art school. I had no interest in film. I would go to a film sometimes, but I really just wanted to paint.

One day I was sitting in a big studio room at the Pennsylvania Academy of the Fine Arts. The room was divided into little cubicles. I was in my cubicle; it was about three o'clock in the afternoon. And I had a painting going, which was of a garden at night. It had a lot of black, with green plants emerging out of the darkness. All of a sudden, these plants started to move, and I heard a wind. I wasn't taking drugs! I thought, *Oh, how fantastic this is!* And I began to wonder if film could be a way to make paintings move.

At the end of each year, there was an experimental painting and sculpture contest. The year before, I had built something for the contest, and this time I thought: *I'm going to do a moving painting*. I built a sculptured screen—six feet by eight feet—and projected a pretty crudely animated stop-motion film on it. It was called *Six Men Getting Sick*. I thought that was going to be the extent of my film career, because this thing actually cost a fortune to make—two hundred dollars. *I simply can't afford to go down this road,* I thought. But an older student saw the project and commissioned me to build one for his home. And that was what started the ball rolling. After that, I just kept getting green lights. Then little by little—or rather leap by leap—I fell in love with this medium.

Know that all of Nature is but a magic theater,
that the great Mother is the master magician,
and that this whole world is peopled by her many parts.
UPANISHADS

It's so magical—I don't know why—to go into a theater and have the lights go down. It's very quiet, and then the curtains start to open. Maybe they're red. And you go into a world.

It's beautiful when it's a shared experience. It's still beautiful when you're at home and your theater is in front of you, though it's not quite as good. It's best on a big screen. That's the way to go into a world.

CINEMA

Cinema is a language. It can say things—big, abstract things. And I love that about it.

I'm not always good with words. Some people are poets and have a beautiful way of saying things with words. But cinema is its own language. And with it you can say so many things, because you've got time and sequences. You've got dialogue. You've got music. You've got sound effects. You have so many tools. And so you can express a feeling and a thought that can't be conveyed any other way. It's a magical medium.

For me, it's so beautiful to think about these pictures and sounds flowing together in time and in sequence, making something that can be done only through cinema. It's not just words or music—it's a whole range of elements coming together and making something that didn't exist before. It's telling stories. It's devising a world, an experience, that people cannot have unless they see that film.

When I catch an idea for a film, I fall in love with the way cinema can express it. I like a story that holds abstractions, and that's what cinema can do.

INTERPRETATION

A film should stand on its own. It's absurd if a filmmaker needs to say what a film means in words. The world in the film is a created one, and people sometimes love going into that world. For them that world is real. And if people find out certain things about how something was done, or how this means this or that means that, the next time they see the film, these things enter into the experience. And then the film becomes different. I think it's so precious and important to maintain that world and not say certain things that could break the experience.

You don't need anything outside of the work. There have been a lot of great books written, and the authors are long since dead, and you can't dig them up. But you've got that book, and a book can make you dream and make you think about things.

People sometimes say they have trouble understanding a film, but I think they understand much more than they realize. Because we're all blessed with intuition—we really have the gift of intuiting things.

Someone might say, I don't understand music; but most people experience music emotionally and would agree that music is an abstraction. You don't need to put music into words right away—you just listen.

Cinema is a lot like music. It can be very abstract, but people have a yearning to make intellectual sense of it, to put it right into words. And when they can't do that, it feels frustrating. But they can come up with an explanation from within, if they just allow it. If they started talking to their friends, soon they would see things—what something is and what something isn't. And they might agree with their friends or argue with their friends—but how could they agree or argue if they don't already know? The interesting thing is, they really do know more than they think. And by voicing what they know, it becomes clearer. And when they see something, they could try to clarify that a little more and, again, go back and forth with a friend. And they would come to some conclusion. And that would be valid.

THE CIRCLE

I like the saying: "The world is as you are." And I think films are as you are. That's why, although the frames of a film are always the same—the same number, in the same sequence, with the same sounds—every screening is different. The difference is sometimes subtle but it's there. It depends on the audience. There is a circle that goes from the audience to the film and back. Each person is looking and thinking and feeling and coming up with his or her own sense of things. And it's probably different from what I fell in love with.

So you don't know how it's going to hit people. But if you thought about how it's going to hit people, or if it's going to hurt someone, or if it's going to do this or do that, then you would have to stop making films. You just do these things that you fall in love with, and you never know what's going to happen.

IDEAS

An idea is a thought. It's a thought that holds more than you think it does when you receive it. But in that first moment there is a spark. In a comic strip, if someone gets an idea, a lightbulb goes on. It happens in an instant, just as in life.

It would be great if the entire film came all at once. But it comes, for me, in fragments. That first fragment is like the Rosetta Stone. It's the piece of the puzzle that indicates the rest. It's a hopeful puzzle piece.

In *Blue Velvet*, it was red lips, green lawns, and the song—Bobby Vinton's version of "Blue Velvet." The next thing was an ear lying in a field. And that was it.

You fall in love with the first idea, that little tiny piece. And once you've got it, the rest will come in time.

DESIRE

Desire for an idea is like bait. When you're fishing, you have to have patience. You bait your hook, and then you wait. The desire is the bait that pulls those fish in—those ideas.

The beautiful thing is that when you catch one fish that you love, even if it's a little fish—a fragment of an idea—that fish will draw in other fish, and they'll hook onto it. Then you're on your way. Soon there are more and more and more fragments, and the whole thing emerges. But it starts with desire.

CONSCIOUSNESS

Through meditation one realizes the unbounded.

That which is unbounded is happy.

There is no happiness in the small.

UPANISHADS

Little fish swim on the surface, but the big ones swim down below. If you can expand the container you're fishing in—your consciousness—you can catch bigger fish.

Here's how it works: Inside every human being is an ocean of pure, vibrant consciousness. When you "transcend" in Transcendental Meditation, you dive down into that ocean of pure consciousness. You splash into it. And it's bliss. You can vibrate with this bliss. Experiencing pure consciousness enlivens it, expands it. It starts to unfold and grow.

If you have a golf-ball-sized consciousness, when you read a book, you'll have a golf-ball-sized understanding; when you look out a window, a golf-ball-sized awareness; when you wake up in the morning, a golf-ball-sized wakefulness; and as you go about your day, a golf-ball-sized inner happiness.

But if you can expand that consciousness, make it grow, then when you read that book, you'll have more understanding; when you look out, more awareness; when you wake up, more wakefulness; and as you go about your day, more inner happiness.

You can catch ideas at a deeper level. And creativity really flows. It makes life more like a fantastic game.

To me, every film, every project, is an experiment. How do you translate this idea? How do you translate it so that it goes from an idea to a film or to a chair? You've got this idea, and you can see it and hear it and feel it and know it. Now, let's say you start cutting a piece of wood and it's just not exactly right. That makes you think more, so you can take off from that. You're now acting and reacting. So it's kind of an experiment to get it all to feel correct.

When you meditate, that flow increases. Action and reaction go faster. You'll get an idea here, then you'll go there, and then there. It's like an improvisational dance. You'll just be zipping along; you'll be banging on all eight cylinders.

And it's not a pretend thing; it's not a feel-good program, where they tell you, "Stop and smell the roses, and your life will get better." It comes from within. It has to start from deep within, and grow and grow and grow. Then things really change.

So transcend, experience the Self—pure consciousness—and watch what happens.

I came to Los Angeles from Philadelphia, where I had lived for five years, attending art school. Philadelphia is known as the City of Brotherly Love, but when I was there, it was a hellhole. There wasn't a lot of love in that city.

I arrived in L.A. at night, so it wasn't until the next morning, when I stepped out of a small apartment on San Vicente Boulevard, that I saw this light. And it thrilled my soul. I feel lucky to live with that light.

I love Los Angeles. I know a lot of people go there and they see just a huge sprawl of sameness. But when you're there for a while, you realize that each section has its own mood. The golden age of cinema is still alive there, in the smell of jasmine at night and the beautiful weather. And the light is inspiring and energizing. Even with smog, there's something about that light that's not harsh, but bright and smooth. It fills me with the feeling that all possibilities are available. I don't know why. It's different from the light in other places. The light in Philadelphia, even in the summer, is not nearly as bright. It was the light that brought everybody to L.A. to make films in the early days. It's still a beautiful place.

Eraserhead is my most spiritual movie. No one understands when I say that, but it is.

Eraserhead was growing in a certain way, and I didn't know what it meant. I was looking for a key to unlock what these sequences were saying. Of course, I understood some of it; but I didn't know the thing that just pulled it all together. And it was a struggle. So I got out my Bible and I started reading. And one day, I read a sentence. And I closed the Bible, because that was it; that was it. And then I saw the thing as a whole. And it fulfilled this vision for me, 100 percent.

I don't think I'll ever say what that sentence was.

THE PACE OF LIFE

Fifty years ago, people were saying, "Everything's speeding up." Twenty years ago, they were still saying, "Everything's speeding up." It always seems that way. And it seems even more so now. It's crazy. When you watch a lot of TV and read a lot of magazines, it can seem like the whole world is passing you by.

When I was making *Eraserhead*, which took five years to complete, I thought I was dead. I thought the world would be so different before it was over. I told myself, *Here I am, locked in this thing. I can't finish it. The world is leaving me behind.* I had stopped listening to music, and I never watched TV anyway. I didn't want to hear stories about what was going on, because hearing these things felt like dying.

At one time, I actually thought of building a small figure of the character Henry, maybe eight inches tall, and constructing a small set out of cardboard, and just stop-motioning him through and finishing it. That was the only way I could figure doing it, because I didn't have any money.

Then, one night, my younger brother and my father sat me down in a kind of dark living room. My brother is very responsible, as is my father. They had a little chat with me. It almost broke my heart, because they said I should get a job and forget *Eraserhead*. I had a little girl, and I should be responsible and get a job.

Well, I did get a job: I delivered the *Wall Street Journal*, and I made fifty dollars a week. I would save up enough to shoot a scene and I eventually finished the whole thing. And I started meditating. Jack Nance, the actor who played Henry, waited three years for me, holding this thought of Henry, keeping it alive. There's a scene in which Jack's character is on one side of a door, and it wasn't until a year and a half later that we filmed him coming through the other side of the door. I wondered, how could this happen? How could it hang together for so long? But Jack waited and held the character.

There's an expression: "Keep your eye on the doughnut, not on the hole." If you keep your eye on the doughnut and do your work, that's all you can control. You can't control any of what's out there, outside yourself. But you can get inside and do the best you can do.

The world *isn't* going to pass you by. There's no guarantee that meditation or delivering the *Wall Street Journal* is going to make you a success. But with focus and with meditation—although the events of your outer life may stay the same—the way you go through those events changes and gets so much better.

YOGIS

When I first saw pictures in books of yogis sitting cross-legged in the woods in the forests of India, something would make me look twice. I'd notice their faces. And it wasn't the face of a man wasting time. It was the face of a man holding something that I not only wanted, but I didn't know about. I was drawn to it. There was such a presence of power and dignity—and an absence of fear. Many of their countenances held playfulness or love, or power and strength.

That made me think that enlightenment must be something real, even though I didn't know what it was. I figured the only way to try for it was to start diving within and see what unfolded. Because I knew that wasn't going to happen with life on the surface in L.A.

BOB'S BIG BOY

'

I used to go to Bob's Big Boy restaurant just about every day from the mid-seventies until the early eighties. I'd have a milk shake and sit and think.

There's a safety in thinking in a diner. You can have your coffee or your milk shake, and you can go off into strange dark areas, and always come back to the safety of the diner.

The Angriest Dog in the World strip came about when I was working on *Eraserhead*. I drew a little dog. And it looked angry. And I started looking at it and thinking about it, and I wondered why it was angry.

And then I did a four-block strip with the dog never moving—three panels were set in the day and one was at night. So there's a passage of time, but the dog never moves. And it struck me that it's the environment that's causing this anger—it's what's going on in the environment. He hears things coming from the house. Or something happens on the other side of the fence, or some kind of weather condition.

It finally boiled down more to what he hears from inside the house. And that seemed like an interesting concept. That it would just be balloons of dialogue from within the house with the dog outside. And what was said in the balloons might conjure a laugh.

The *L.A. Weekly* wanted to publish it. So they published it for nine years. After a couple of years, it was in the *Baltimore Sun* as well. Every Monday I had to come up with what to say. Then I would phone it in. I wouldn't always do the lettering and sometimes I didn't like the way the lettering looked, so toward the end I did some of the lettering again.

The editor who had taken on the cartoon went off to another paper partway through the run, and I had different editors. Toward the end of the nine years, the same editor who had taken it on came back to that paper. And he asked me not to do it anymore. It had run its course.

MUSIC

I was listening to the radio one day when I was working on *The Elephant Man*, and I heard Samuel Barber's Adagio for Strings. I fell in love with this piece for the last scene of the film. I asked Jonathan Sanger, the producer, to get it. And he came back with nine different records. I listened to them, and I said, "No, that's not what I heard at all." All nine were completely wrong. So he went out and bought more. Finally I heard André Previn's version, and I said, "That's it." It was composed of the same notes as the others, of course, but it was the *way* he did it.

The music has to marry with the picture and enhance it. You can't just lob something in and think it's going to work, even if it's one of your all-time favorite songs. That piece of music may have nothing to do with the scene. When it marries, you can *feel* it. The thing jumps; a "whole is greater than the sum of the parts" kind of thing can happen.

INTUITION

Know That by knowing which everything is known.

UPANISHADS

Life is filled with abstractions, and the only way we make heads or tails of it is through intuition. Intuition is seeing the solution—seeing it, knowing it. It's emotion and intellect going together. That's essential for the filmmaker.

How do you get something to feel right? Everybody's got the same tools: the camera and the tapes and the world and actors. But in putting those parts together, there are differences. That's where intuition enters.

Personally, I think intuition can be sharpened and expanded through meditation, diving into the Self. There's an ocean of consciousness inside each of us, and it's an ocean of solutions. When you dive into that ocean, that consciousness, you enliven it.

You don't dive for specific solutions; you dive to enliven that ocean of consciousness. Then your intuition grows and you have a way of solving those problems—knowing when it's not quite right and knowing a way to make it feel correct for you. That capacity grows and things go much more smoothly.

One unbounded ocean of consciousness became light, water,
and matter. And the three became many. In this way the
whole universe was created as an unbounded ocean of
consciousness ever unfolding within itself.

UPANISHADS

The ocean of pure consciousness that Maharishi Mahesh Yogi talks about is also known by modern science as the Unified Field.

When Maharishi first arrived in the United States in 1959, the Unified Field from quantum physics hadn't yet been discovered. So people would say, "Oh, that's baloney—they're looking for some field at the base of everything, but it doesn't really exist; no one knows if it's true." But then, about thirty years ago, quantum physics discovered this field. They discovered it by going into matter, deeper and deeper and deeper, and one day, there it was: the Unified Field. And then scientists like Dr. John Hagelin said that it's true: Every single thing that is a thing emerges from this field.

So modern science and ancient science are coming together.

Vedic science—the science of consciousness—studies the laws of nature, the constitution of the universe, and how it all unfolds. In Vedic science, this ocean of pure consciousness is called *Atma*, the Self. "Know thy Self." Well, how? You don't know yourself by looking in the mirror. You don't know yourself by sitting down and having a talk with yourself. But it's there, within, within, within.

Transcendental Meditation is a simple, easy, effortless technique that allows any human being to dive within, to experience subtler levels of mind and intellect, and to enter this ocean of pure consciousness, the Unified Field—*the Self*.

It's not the intellectual understanding of the field but the experiencing of it that does everything. You dive within, and by experiencing this field of pure consciousness, you enliven it; you unfold it; it grows. And the final outcome of this growth of consciousness is called enlightenment, which is the full potential for us all.

Many people have already experienced transcending, but they may not realize it. It's an experience that you can have just before you go to sleep. You're awake, but you experience a sort of fall, and you maybe see some white light and get a little jolt of bliss. And you say, "Holy jumping George!" When you go from one state of consciousness to another—for instance, from waking to sleeping—you pass through a gap. And in that gap, you can transcend.

I picture it like a round white room that has yellow, red, and blue curtains covering the white wall. The curtains are three states of consciousness: waking, sleeping, and dreaming. But in the gap between each curtain, you can see the white of the Absolute—the pure bliss consciousness. You can transcend in that little piece of white. Then you come to the next state of consciousness. The white room really is all around you all the time, even though the curtains cover most of it; so it's here, there, and everywhere. And sometimes, without knowing it or knowing how, people have transcended. With Transcendental Meditation, from the waking state of consciousness you can experience that white wall anytime when you sit and meditate. That's the beautiful thing about it.

That Atma alone, that state of simplest form of awareness alone,
is worthy of seeing, hearing, contemplating, and realizing.
UPANISHADS

Some forms of meditation are just contemplation or concentration: they'll keep you on the surface. You won't transcend; you won't get that fourth state of consciousness and you won't get that bliss. You'll stay on the surface.

Relaxation techniques can take you a little way in. That's beautiful; it's like having a massage. But it's not transcending. Transcending is its own unique thing.

When you dive within, the Self is there and true happiness is there. There's a pure, huge, unbounded ocean of it. It's bliss—physical, emotional, mental, and spiritual happiness that starts growing from within. And all those things that used to *kill* you diminish. In the film business, there's so much pressure; there's so much room for anxiety and fear. But transcending makes life more like a game—a fantastic game. And creativity can really flow. It's an ocean of creativity. It's the same creativity that creates everything that is a thing. It's us.

And why is it so easy? Because it's the nature of the mind, because the mind wants to go to fields of greater happiness. It just naturally wants to go. And the deeper you go, the more there is of that until you hit 100 percent pure bliss. Transcendental Meditation is the vehicle that takes you there. But it's that experiencing of the ocean of pure bliss consciousness that does everything.

Scientifically, more and more is coming out to show that transcending is real and its benefits are real. By measuring EEG patterns in brain research, they can prove that someone is transcending; they can prove that the person is experiencing a fourth state of consciousness. I've seen this in live demonstrations traveling with neuroscientist Dr. Fred Travis.

When you work on music, you use a certain part of your brain. When you talk, you use another part. When you sing, you use a different part. When you do mathematics, you use still another part. But if you want to use your full brain, you need to transcend. And then every time you transcend, you carry a little bit more of that transcendental consciousness as you work on your mathematic problems, as you sing, or what have you. Your brain is holding this coherence no matter what you do.

It's a holistic experience; it's total brain functioning. And that increasingly becomes a permanent state the more you experience the Unified Field, the more that consciousness grows. It doesn't happen overnight, but it happens more and more each day. Vedic science has always said that this field is there and that you can experience it. And now modern science, with each step forward, is affirming that.

You can meditate anywhere. You can meditate in an airport, at work, anywhere you happen to be.

Usually, I meditate in the morning before breakfast, and in the evening before dinner. But when I'm shooting, I meditate before I go, and again at lunch. And if I haven't meditated long enough, I'll meditate when I finish.

I've been in places where there are no other meditators around, but it's very surprising: people kind of like it. I'll ask for a quiet room, and they say, "Oh, yes, yes, I'll find you a very nice, quiet place, and protect you." And I go in and meditate away.

We waste so much time on other things, anyway. Once you add this and have a routine, it fits in very naturally.

IDENTITY

The thing about meditation is: You become more and more *you*.

I love the French. They're the biggest film buffs and protectors of cinema in the world. They really look out for the filmmaker and the rights of the filmmaker, and they believe in final cut. I've been very lucky that I've been in with some French companies that have backed me.

But it wasn't always that way. When I made *Dune*, I didn't have final cut. It was a huge, huge sadness, because I felt I had sold out, and on top of that, the film was a failure at the box office. If you do what you believe in and have a failure, that's one thing: you can still live with yourself. But if you don't, it's like dying twice. It's very, very painful.

It's totally absurd for filmmakers not to be able to make films the way they want to make them. But in this business it's very common.

I came from painting. And a painter has none of those worries. A painter paints a painting. No one comes in and says, "You've got to change that blue." It's a joke to think that a film is going to mean anything if somebody else fiddles with it. If they give you the right to make the film, they owe you the right to make it the way you think it should be. The filmmaker should decide on every single element, every single word, every single sound, every single thing going down that highway through time. Otherwise, it won't hold together. The film may suck, but at least you made it suck on your own.

So for me, *Dune* was a huge failure. I knew I was getting into trouble when I agreed not to have final cut. I was hoping it would work out, but it didn't. The end result is not what I wanted, and that's a sadness.

Here's the thing, though. When you meditate and bliss starts coming up inside, it is not as painful. You can ride through things like this and live through it. But it has killed a lot of people. It has made them not want to make a film again.

THERAPY

I went to a psychiatrist once. I was doing something that had become a pattern in my life, and I thought, *Well, I should go talk to a psychiatrist.* When I got into the room, I asked him, "Do you think that this process could, in any way, damage my creativity?" And he said, "Well, David, I have to be honest: it could." And I shook his hand and left.

I love dream logic; I just like the way dreams go. But I have hardly ever gotten ideas from dreams. I get more ideas from music, or from just walking around.

On *Blue Velvet*, though, I was really struggling with the script. I wrote four different drafts. And I had some problems with it near the end. Then one day, I was in an office and I was supposed to go in and meet somebody in the next office. A secretary was there, and I asked her if I could have a piece of paper, because I suddenly remembered that the night before I'd had this dream. And there it was. There were three little elements that solved those problems. That's the only time that's happened.

I met Angelo Badalamenti on *Blue Velvet* and since then he has composed music for all my films. He's like my brother.

The way we work is: I like to sit next to him on the piano bench. I talk and Angelo plays. He plays my words. But sometimes he doesn't understand my words, so he plays very badly. Then I say, "No, no, no, no, Angelo." And I change my words a little bit, and he plays differently. And then I say, "No, no, no, no, Angelo," and I change my words. And somehow through this process he will catch something, and I'll say, "That's it!" And then he starts going with his magic, down that correct path. It's so much fun. If Angelo lived next door to me, I'd like to do this every day. But he lives in New Jersey, and I live in Los Angeles.

SOUND

Sometimes you hear a piece of music, and it marries to a scene in the script. When I'm shooting, I will often play that piece of music in the headphones while listening to the dialogue. Hearing the music is just a verification that things are going the right way—for instance, the right pace or lighting. It's just another tool to ensure that you're following that original idea and being true to it. So it's a good thing if you've got some music up front to play to see if the scene works.

Sound is so important to the feel of a film. To get the right presence for a room, the right feel from the outside, or the right-sounding dialogue is like playing a musical instrument. You have to do a lot of experimenting to get that just right. It usually happens after the film is cut. But I'm always trying to gather what I call "firewood." So I have piles of things I can go to and see if they'll work. You just have to pop one sound in, and you realize right away, *Oh, that is not working*.

It doesn't matter how wonderful an actor is; when you're casting, you have to pick the person who marries to that part, who can do that part.

I don't ever give actors cold readings. I feel that's a torment for them, and I don't learn anything. Plus, then I would want to start rehearsing with them. It would take a long, long time to do that with every actor. So I like to just talk with them and look at them while they talk. I start running them through the script in my head as they're talking. Some of them go partway and then stop. Then one of them will go all the way through, and I'll know.

On *Blue Velvet*, I worked with a casting director, Johanna Ray. And we had all brought up Dennis Hopper. But everybody said, "No, no; you can't work with Dennis. He's really in bad shape, and you'll have nothing but trouble." So we continued looking for people. But one day, Dennis's agent called and said that Dennis was clean and sober and had already done another picture, and I could talk to that director to verify it. Then Dennis called and said, "I *have* to play Frank, because I *am* Frank." That thrilled me, and scared me.

Sometimes, I'll have somebody in mind from the beginning. There's a character in *Mulholland Drive* that worked that way. It was about seven-thirty in the evening, and I was dictating to my assistant—this beautiful woman. And I started talking in a funny way. I started talking like the cowboy in *Mulholland Drive*. He just came walking out. I realized, after I'd gone on for a while, that my friend Monty Montgomery would be perfect for that. And he's not even an actor. Though he is an actor, really; he's a very great actor. But he married to that part.

There are some actors I return to—Kyle MacLachlan, for instance. I like Kyle, and maybe he's kind of an alter ego. But the rule of thumb, obviously, is to get the right person for that role. And that's what you go for. So the thing is, even though Kyle is my friend, if he's not right for the part, unfortunately he doesn't get that part.

What's also really interesting is that when you work with somebody, you pick that person for a particular role. But then, during lunch or something, you see another side of that person. And you remember that. So if there's another role that comes up, and somebody says, "Well, Kyle couldn't do that," you may remember this side of him and say, "Yes, he could."

When you rehearse, it doesn't matter where you start. You get your actors together and you just pick a scene that defines the characters in your mind. You have the rehearsal, and wherever it is, it is. The thing may be all over the place.

Then you talk. Often the talking doesn't appear to make much sense. But it does to me and to whomever I'm talking with. You can feel it making sense. So the next time you rehearse, things may be a little closer. And closer still the next time.

There's a lot of talking, especially at first. You can say many things, sometimes strange and stupid words. But you develop these little codes with certain actors or actresses. For me, for example, "more wind" means "more mystery." It's a weird thing. Yet little by little, just by moving your hand or saying some word, a person says, "Ah, ah, okay." And actors, at a certain point in early rehearsals, catch on. Then they're rolling. And all their talent can go down the right track.

The same holds with everyone you work with. When people say "rehearsal," they're usually talking only about actors. But there's a rehearsal that goes on with all the people of the crew, in every department. The idea is to get everybody to come together and go down the same track—the track indicated by the ideas.

So a prop man, for instance, may bring a bunch of props, and they're totally wrong, but you say a few things, and he says, "Oh, okay," and he comes back, and now he's much closer. And then you say a few more words, and then he goes back, and now he's bringing the perfect things. It's a matter of talking and action and reaction.

It works the same way with all departments, because every element of the film is crucial if the whole is going to hold together. It's always the same kind of process. You start rehearsing, and it doesn't matter how far away things are. Just start. And you may say, "Oh, my goodness—we're very far away." (You say that internally, of course!) Then you start talking and rehearsing. And it begins getting closer and closer and closer. It's an abstract sort of thing, but everybody is getting there. The lightbulb goes off at one point in each person. And they say, "I think I've got it." Then you have another rehearsal. And you don't want to kill the thing, so you leave it alone until you begin shooting.

You're always thinking of that original idea—the mood, the character. And through talking, rehearsing, talking, rehearsing, pretty soon it comes. And once everyone catches that drift, they're rolling down the line with you, and they're flowing with the things that were in the original idea. That's how it works.

I hear stories about directors who scream at actors, or they trick them somehow to get a performance. And there are some people who try to run the whole business on fear. But I think this is such a joke—it's pathetic and stupid at the same time.

When people are in fear, they don't want to go to work. So many people today have that feeling. Then the fear starts turning into hate, and they begin to hate going to work. Then the hate can turn into anger and people can become angry at their boss and their work.

If I ran my set with fear, I would get 1 percent, not 100 percent, of what I get. And there would be no fun in going down the road together. And it *should* be fun. In work and in life, we're all supposed to get along. We're supposed to have so much fun, like puppy dogs with our tails wagging. It's supposed to be great living; it's supposed to be fantastic.

Instead of instilling fear, if a company offered a way for everyone in the business to dive within—to start expanding energy and intelligence—people would work overtime for free. They would be far more creative. And the company would just leap forward. This is the way it can be. It's not the way it is, but it could be that way so easily.

When you work, you want a happy crew going down the road together. You need the ability to focus on things as a group. You need to concentrate on one thing at a time and not have a million different things distracting you. This capacity grows when people start meditating and diving within.

There's an expression: "Where the attention is, that becomes lively." So when you focus on a thing, it's almost as if you start it moving and vibrating. You say, "This is what we're going to do today, this is where we are, and this is what we want to accomplish." Then the work gets better and the group gets happier.

Ideas come along in the strangest way when you just pay attention. And sometimes things happen on the set that make you start dreaming.

When we were shooting the pilot for *Twin Peaks*, we had a set dresser named Frank Silva. Frank was never destined to be in *Twin Peaks*, never in a million years. But we were shooting in Laura Palmer's home and Frank was moving some furniture around in her room. I was in the hall, underneath a fan. And a woman said, "Frank, don't move that dresser in front of the door like that. Don't lock yourself in the room."

And this picture came to me of Frank in the room. I went running in and I asked Frank, "Are you an actor?" And he said, "Well, yes, I happen to be," because everyone in L.A. is an actor. And maybe everyone in the world. So I said, "Frank, you're going to be in this scene."

We did a pan shot of the room, twice without Frank and then one time with Frank frozen at the base of the bed. But I didn't know what it was for or what it meant.

That evening, we went downstairs and we were shooting Laura Palmer's mother on the couch. She was lying there in sadness and torment. Suddenly she sees something in her mind's eye and bolts upright, screaming. Sean, the camera operator, had to turn the wheels and follow her face as she bolted up. And it looked to me like he did a perfect job. So I said, "Cut—perfect, beautiful!" And Sean said, "No, no, no. It's not."

"What is it?"

"There was someone reflected in the mirror."

"Who was reflected in the mirror?"

"Frank was reflected in the mirror."

So things like this happen and make you start dreaming. And one thing leads to another, and if you let it, a whole other thing opens up.

I love going into another world, and I love mysteries. So I don't really like to know very much ahead of time. I like the feeling of discovery. I think that's one of the great things about a continuing story: that you can go in, and go deeper and deeper and deeper. You begin to feel the mystery, and things start coming.

The popularity of continuing stories on TV goes in waves. Periodically, the networks do these polls. And they come up with different things—at one time they had determined that people don't watch every single week. People may watch two times a month and, so the reasoning went, they lose their way in a continuing story and drop away from the show. Obviously, the networks don't want people to drop away, so for a certain period of time they soured on a continuing story and wanted closed endings.

I don't know quite how the network decided to let *Twin Peaks* become a pilot. But just because they let something become a pilot, it doesn't mean they're going to make it into a series. So it got that far. And even then, they didn't really know what to do with it. They send these things to a place; I think it's in Philadelphia. And they have people watch the shows and grade them. Somehow, it got a fairly good score, but not spectacular. I don't know what happened between that time and the time it aired, but it just got a huge, huge share that opening night. So that was a very lucky thing.

One summer day, I was at a laboratory called Consolidated Film Industries in Los Angeles. We were editing the pilot for *Twin Peaks* and had finished for the day. It was around six-thirty in the evening and we had gone outside. There were cars in the parking lot. I leaned my hands on the roof of one car, and it was very, very warm— not hot, but nicely warm. I was leaning there and—*ssssst!*—the Red Room appeared. And the backward thing appeared, and then some of the dialogue.

So I had this idea, these fragments. And I fell in love with them.

That's how it starts. The idea tells you to build this Red Room. So you think about it. "Wait a minute," you say, "the walls are red, but they're not hard walls." Then you think some more. "They're curtains. And they're not opaque; they're translucent." Then you put these curtains there. "But the floor. . . it needs something." And you go back to the idea and there was something on the floor—it was all there. So you do this thing on the floor. And you start to remember the idea more. You try some things and you make mistakes, but you rearrange, add other stuff, and then it feels the way that idea felt.

ASK THE IDEA

The form which embodies that which appeared in
consciousness—that is to be held within consciousness.

UPANISHADS

The idea is the whole thing. If you stay true to the idea, it tells you everything you need to know, really. You just keep working to make it look like that idea looked, feel like it felt, sound like it sounded, and be the way it was. And it's weird, because when you veer off, you sort of *know* it. You know when you're doing something that is not correct because it *feels* incorrect. It says, "No, no; this isn't like the idea said it was." And when you're getting into it the correct way, it feels correct. It's an intuition: You feel-think your way through. You start one place, and as you go, it gets more and more finely tuned. But all along it's the idea talking. At some point, it feels correct to you. And you hope that it feels somewhat correct to others.

Sometimes, I'll go into a set that was built based on an idea, and for a moment or so, I think I am right in that idea. It's fantastic. But a lot of times, you don't build the set; you find a location that feels correct, based on that idea. And the location can be changed in many ways to get closer to the idea. The props and the light can be altered. The light can play a huge role in this. And you just keep working and working until the thing feels correct, based on the idea. If you pay attention to all the elements swimming together, then lo and behold, at the very end, it's surprising how close it all is to that original spark.

New ideas can come along during the process, too. And a film isn't finished until it's finished, so you're always on guard. Sometimes those happy accidents occur. They may even be the last pieces of the puzzle that allow it all to come together. And you feel so thankful: *How in the world did this happen?*

During *Blue Velvet*, we were shooting a scene in the apartment of the character Ben, who is played by Dean Stockwell. At a certain point, Dean was going to sing "In Dreams" by Roy Orbison. He was going to lip-sync to that and sing it to Dennis Hopper. In the script, he was supposed to pick up a small lamp from a table and use it as a microphone.

But right in front of him on the set—and Patricia Norris, the production designer, said she did not put it there—was this work lamp. It had a long cord and its bulb was hidden from the audience, but illuminated Dean's face. And Dean just snatched this up. He thought it was placed there for him. There's so many of these things that come along.

Sometimes accidents happen that aren't happy, but you have to work with those as well. You adapt. You throw out this thing, and throw out that thing, and throw out another thing. But if you pay attention to the original idea—stay true to that—it's surprising how, at the end, even the things that were accidents are honest. They're true to the idea.

TEST AUDIENCE

Although you can't make a film with the audience in mind, at a certain point, before it's finished, you need to experience the film with a group. Sometimes you lose your objectivity a little, and you need to get a feel for what's working and what isn't. That can be the worst screening—very close to hell on earth. But, again, the film's not finished until it's finished.

After you screen it for that group, for the sake of the whole, certain things may have to be cut down or some things may need to be added. They're not exactly mistakes. Some of the scenes that are removed from a film are kind of nice scenes on their own. But to let the whole thing work, they have to go. It's part of the process—it always happens to some degree.

It's dangerous, I think, to say that a woman in a film represents all women, or a man in a film represents all men. Some critics love generalizations. But it's *that* particular character in *this* particular story going down *that* particular road. Those specific things make their own world. And sometimes it's a world that we'd like to go into and experience.

DARKNESS

People have asked me why—if meditation is so great and gives you so much bliss—are my films so dark, and there's so much violence?

There are many, many dark things flowing around in this world now, and most films reflect the world in which we live. They're stories. Stories are always going to have conflict. They're going to have highs and lows, and good and bad.

I fall in love with certain ideas. And I am where I am. Now, if I told you I was enlightened, and this is enlightened filmmaking, that would be another story. But I'm just a guy from Missoula, Montana, doing my thing, going down the road like everybody else.

We all reflect the world we live in. Even if you make a period film, it will reflect your times. You can see the way period films differ, depending on when they were made. It's a sensibility—how they talk, certain themes—and those things change as the world changes.

And so, even though I'm from Missoula, Montana, which is not the surrealistic capital of the world, you could be anywhere and see a kind of strangeness in how the world is these days, or have a certain way of looking at things.

SUFFERING

It's good for the artist to understand conflict and stress. Those things can give you ideas. But I guarantee you, if you have enough stress, you won't be able to create. And if you have enough conflict, it will just get in the way of your creativity. You can understand conflict, but you don't have to live in it.

In stories, in the worlds that we can go into, there's suffering, confusion, darkness, tension, and anger. There are murders; there's all kinds of stuff. But the filmmaker doesn't have to *be* suffering to *show* suffering. You can show it, show the human condition, show conflicts and contrasts, but you don't have to go through that yourself. You are the orchestrator of it, but you're not in it. Let your characters do the suffering.

It's common sense: The more the artist is suffering, the less creative he is going to be. It's less likely that he is going to enjoy his work and less likely that he will be able to do really good work.

Right here people might bring up Vincent van Gogh as an example of a painter who did great work in spite of—or because of—his suffering. I like to think that van Gogh would have been even more prolific and even greater if he wasn't so restricted by the things tormenting him. I don't think it was pain that made him so great—I think his painting brought him whatever happiness he had.

Some artists believe that anger, depression, or these negative things give them an edge. They think they need to hold on to that anger and fear so they can put it in their work. And they don't like the idea of getting happy—it makes them want to puke. They think it would make them lose their edge or their power.

But you will not lose your edge if you meditate. You will not lose your creativity. And you will not lose your power. In fact, the more you meditate and transcend, the more those things will grow, and you'll know it. You will gain far more understanding of all aspects of life when you dive within. In that way, understanding grows, appreciation grows, the bigger picture forms, and the human condition becomes more and more visible.

If you're an artist, you've got to *know* about anger without being restricted by it. In order to create, you've got to have energy; you've got to have clarity. You've got to be able to catch ideas. You've got to be strong enough to fight unbelievable pressure and stress in this world. So it just makes sense to nurture the place where that strength and clarity and energy come from—to dive in and enliven that. It's a strange thing, but it's true in my experience: Bliss is like a flak jacket. It's a protecting thing. If you have enough bliss, it's invincibility. And when those negative things start lifting, you can catch more ideas and see them with greater understanding. You can get fired up more easily. You've got more energy, more clarity. Then you can really go to work and translate those ideas into one medium or another.

He who sees everything as nothing but the Self,

and the Self in everything he sees,

such a seer withdraws from nothing.

For the enlightened, all that exists is nothing but the Self,

so how could any suffering or delusion continue

for those who know this Oneness?

UPANISHADS

Negativity is like darkness. So what is darkness? You look at darkness, and you see that it's really nothing: It's the absence of something. You turn on the light, and darkness goes.

But sunlight, for instance, doesn't get rid of negativity. It gets rid of darkness, but not negativity. So what light can you turn on that removes negativity the way sunlight removes darkness? It's the light of pure consciousness, the Self—the light of unity.

Don't fight the darkness. Don't even worry about the darkness. Turn on the light and the darkness goes. Turn up that light of pure consciousness: Negativity goes.

Now you say, "That sounds so sweet." It sounds *too* sweet. But it's a real thing.

Just as a mirror shines bright once it has been cleaned of dust,

so those who have seen the Self shine in mind and body.

They are always and forever filled with happiness.

UPANISHADS

How does meditation get rid of negativity?

Picture it this way: You are the Empire State Building. You've got hundreds of rooms. And in those rooms, there's a lot of junk. And *you* put all that junk there. Now you take this elevator, which is going to be the dive within. And you go down below the building; you go to the Unified Field beneath the building—pure consciousness. And it's like electric gold. You experience that. And that electric gold activates these little cleaning robots. They start going, and they start cleaning the rooms. They put in gold where the dirt and junk and garbage were. These stresses that were in there like coils of barbed wire can unwind. They evaporate, they come out. You're cleaning and infusing simultaneously. You're on the road to a beautiful state of enlightenment.

I was raised Presbyterian. I respect people who are religious, and I think they find something there that's beautiful, just beautiful. There's truth there. Because these religions are old, though, and they've been fiddled with, possibly, I feel some of the original keys from the masters have been lost. But we're all going to the same beautiful goal; that's the way I see it.

All religions flow ultimately to the one ocean. Transcendental Meditation is a technique to experience that ocean, and it's a technique practiced by people from all religions. Transcendental Meditation itself is not a religion—it's not against any religion; it's not against anything.

We all want expanded consciousness and bliss. It's a natural, human desire. And a lot of people look for it in drugs. But the problem is that the body, the physiology, takes a hard hit on drugs. Drugs injure the nervous system, so they just make it harder to get those experiences on your own.

I have smoked marijuana, but I no longer do. I went to art school in the 1960s, so you can imagine what was going on. Yet my friends were the ones who said, "No, no, no, David, don't you take those drugs." I was pretty lucky.

Besides, far more profound experiences are available naturally. When your consciousness starts expanding, those experiences are there. All those things can be seen. It's just a matter of expanding that ball of consciousness. And the ball of consciousness can expand to be infinite and unbounded. It's totality. You can have totality. So all those experiences are there for you, without the side effects of drugs.

TURN ON THE LIGHT

In the vicinity of Yoga—unity—
hostile tendencies are eliminated.
YOGA SUTRAS

We're like lightbulbs. If bliss starts growing inside you, it's like a light; it affects the environment.

If you go into a room where someone's been having a big argument, it's not so pleasant. You can feel it. Even if the argument's over, you can feel it. But if you go into a room where someone has just finished meditating, you can feel that bliss. It's very nice to feel that.

We all affect our environments. You enjoy that light inside, and if you ramp it up brighter and brighter, you enjoy more and more of it. And that light will extend out farther and farther.

INDUSTRIAL

SYMPHONY NO. 1

Industrial Symphony No. 1 was the first and only time I've done a stage production. It was at the Brooklyn Academy of Music. We had two weeks to set it up, but only one day in the actual theater to put it all together and do two performances.

I was working on the music with Angelo Badalamenti, and we were attempting some abstract musical things to tie different elements together. I had some people building sets. But from the time the sets went up, the whole thing had to be rehearsed and lit in *one day*.

So the day came, and we had the late morning and afternoon to rehearse and then put on two shows. I wanted to start rehearsing—from the beginning, to rehearse all the way through. We started, and about an hour and a half later, I'd hardly even gotten into the thing, even though it wasn't very long. And I realized that I was facing a gigantic, definite disaster. I thought, *I'm never going to make it unless I get some kind of an idea.* And, bingo—it happened.

Maybe it's not reinventing the wheel—perhaps it's just common sense—but what I did was, I went one by one. I would grab this person and say, "Do you see that, over there? When that man there goes there, and then leaves, then you go there." And he'd say, "Okay." "And when you get there, you do this, this, and this." "Okay." Then I'd go to the next person, and I'd say, "Do you see that man there? When he does this, this, and this, then it's your cue to go over here, and you do that, that, and that." We never had a rehearsal, but fortunately it all worked out.

At the time that Barry Gifford and I were writing the script for *Lost Highway*, I was sort of obsessed with the O. J. Simpson trial. Barry and I never talked about it this way, but I think the film is somehow related to that.

What struck me about O. J. Simpson was that he was able to smile and laugh. He was able to go golfing later with seemingly very few problems about the whole thing. I wondered how, if a person did these deeds, he could go on living. And we found this great psychology term—"psychogenic fugue"—describing an event where the mind tricks itself to escape some horror. So, in a way, *Lost Highway* is about that. And also the fact that nothing can stay hidden forever.

RESTRICTIONS

Sometimes restrictions get the mind going. If you've got tons and tons of money, you may relax and figure you can throw money at any problem that comes along. You don't have to think so hard. But when you have limitations, sometimes you come up with very creative, inexpensive ideas.

My friend Gary D'Amico is a special effects man. And he loves to blow things up. He's the one who blew up the house in *Lost Highway*. And he didn't have the stuff to do it. I didn't even know I was going to blow up that house. The production manager asked, "Are we going to tear the house down? Do you want to save any of the stuff?" And I said, "Tear it down?" And I started thinking. I went to Gary and said, "What if I wanted to blow up something?" His face lit up. And I said, "I want to blow up this house."

And he said, "Oh, I wish you would have told me. I don't know what I've got."

But then he said, "Yeah, yeah—we can do it." And so he went in and wired up this thing with everything he had. And it was the most beautiful sight. If he had brought in what he would have, had he known in advance, it wouldn't have been as beautiful. It was a *soft explosion*. It sent the stuff for hundreds of feet. But softly. And then we shot it backward. So it turned out incredible.

Mulholland Drive was originally going to be a continuing story on television. We shot it as a pilot: open-ended, to make you want to see more and more.

I heard that the man at ABC who was making the decision whether to accept the pilot or not saw it at six a.m. He was watching television across the room while having some coffee and making some phone calls. And he hated what he saw; it bored him. So he turned it down.

Then I had the chance, fortunately, to make it into a feature. But I didn't have the ideas.

Now, you don't use meditation to catch ideas. You're expanding the container, and you come out very refreshed, filled with energy, and raring to go out and catch ideas afterward.

But in this particular case, almost the day I got the go-ahead to turn it into a feature, I went into meditation, and somewhere about ten minutes in, *ssssst!* There it was. Like a string of pearls, the ideas came. And they affected the middle, the beginning, and the end. I felt very blessed. But that's the only time it's happened during meditation.

THE BOX AND THE KEY

I don't have a clue what those are.

A sense of place is so critical in cinema, because you want to go into another world. Every story has its own world, and its own feel, and its own mood. So you try to put together all these things—these little details—to create that sense of place.

It has a lot to do with lighting and sound. The sounds that come into a room can help paint a world there and make it so much fuller. While many sets are good enough for a wide shot, in my mind, they should be good enough for close scrutiny, for the little details to show. You may not ever really see them all, but you've got to feel that they're there, somehow, to feel that it's a real place, a real world.

BEAUTY

When you see an aging building or a rusted bridge, you are seeing nature and man working together. If you paint over a building, there is no more magic to that building. But if it is allowed to age, then man has built it and nature has added into it—it's so organic.

But often people wouldn't think to permit that, except for scenic designers.

TEXTURE

I don't necessarily love rotting bodies, but there's a texture to a rotting body that is unbelievable. Have you ever seen a little rotted animal? I love looking at those things, just as much as I like to look at a close-up of some tree bark, or a small bug, or a cup of coffee, or a piece of pie. You get in close and the textures are wonderful.

Wood is one of the greatest materials to work with. There are soft woods and hard woods, and they all have their own beauty when you are working with them. When I saw through a piece of freshly cut pine, the smell of it just sends me right to heaven. The same goes even for pine needles. I used to chew Ponderosa pine pitch, which is the sap that oozes out of the tree and dries on the outside of the bark. If you can get a fresh piece of pitch, it is like syrup. It will stick to you and you won't be able to get it off your hands. But sometimes it hardens like old honey. And you can chew this, and the flavor of pine pitch will make you crazy, in a good way.

Pine, being a softer wood, is easier to work with and is readily available. When I was young, I did a lot of things with pine. But then, I started falling in love with Douglas fir, vertical-grain Douglas fir. When you varnish a piece of Douglas fir, it has a depth of beauty that is just phenomenal. And then when you put two pieces of wood together, you start realizing there are so many possibilities. And you learn some tricks along the way.

And then there's Günter, a German carpenter, who didn't use electric tools at all. He would just come up to the house with a set of hand tools in a beautiful wooden box with a handle, which he'd carry around. And Günter—I'd watch this man—did little detail work on Douglas fir. He would put these two pieces of wood together, and then he'd rub his old, battered thumbs against the seam—and the seam would disappear. It was like a magic act, the pieces fit so perfectly. Günter was a real carpenter.

Some mornings, in a perfect world, you might wake up, have a coffee, finish meditation, and say, "Okay, today I'm going into the shop to work on a lamp." This idea comes to you, you can see it, but to accomplish it you need what I call a "setup." For example, you may need a working shop or a working painting studio. You may need a working music studio. Or a computer room where you can write something. It's crucial to have a setup, so that, at any given moment, when you get an idea, you have the place and the tools to make it happen.

If you don't have a setup, there are many times when you get the inspiration, the idea, but you have no tools, no place to put it together. And the idea just sits there and festers. Over time, it will go away. You didn't fulfill it—and that's just a heartache.

FIRE

Sitting in front of a fire is mesmerizing. It's magical. I feel the same way about elec-
tricity. And smoke. And flickering lights.

Often, in a scene, the room and the light together signify a mood. So even if the room isn't perfect, you can work with the light and get it to feel correct, so that it has the mood that came with the original idea.

The light can make all the difference in a film, even in a character.

I love seeing people come out of darkness.

I didn't write *The Straight Story*. It was something of a departure for me, because it's completely linear. But then, I fell in love with the emotion of the script. So you can fall in love with something that already exists, too, and it's similar to falling in love with an idea. You get that feeling of what it could be on film, and that guides you.

I am a huge admirer of Billy Wilder. There are two films of his that I most love because they create such a world of their own: *Sunset Boulevard* and *The Apartment*.

And then there's Fellini, who is a tremendous inspiration. I like *La Strada* and *8½*—but really all of them and, again, for the world and the characters and the mood, and for this level, which you can't put your finger on, that comes out in each one.

I love Hitchcock. *Rear Window* is a film that makes me crazy, in a good way. There's such a coziness with James Stewart in one room, and it's such a cool room, and the people who come into this room—Grace Kelly, for instance, and Thelma Ritter—it's just so fantastic that they're all in on a mystery that's unfolding out their window. It's magical and everybody who sees it feels that. It's so nice to go back and visit that place.

I was shooting a commercial in Rome, and I was working with two people who had worked with Fellini. He was in a hospital in northern Italy, but we heard he was being moved down to Rome. So I said, "Do you think it'd be possible to go over and say hello to him?" And they said, "Yeah, we'll try to arrange that." There was an attempt on a Thursday night that fell through, but Friday night, we went over. It was about six o'clock in the evening in summer—a beautiful, warm evening. Two of us went in and were taken into Fellini's room. There was another man in the room and my friend knew him, so he went over and talked to him. Fellini had me sit down. He was in a little wheelchair between the two beds, and he took my hand, and we sat and talked for half an hour. I don't think I asked him much. I just listened a lot. He talked about the old days—how things were. He told stories. I really liked sitting near him. And then we left. That was Friday night, and Sunday he went into a coma and never came out.

Stanley Kubrick is one of my all-time favorite filmmakers, and he did me a great honor early in my career that really encouraged me. I was working on *The Elephant Man*, and I was at Lee International Studios in England, standing in a hallway. One of the producers of *The Elephant Man*, Jonathan Sanger, brought over some guys who were working with George Lucas and said, "They've got a story for you." And I said, "Okay."

They said, "Yesterday, David, we were out at Elstree Studios, and we met Kubrick. And as we were talking to him, he said to us, 'How would you fellas like to come up to my house tonight and see my favorite film?'" They said, "That would be fantastic." They went up, and Stanley Kubrick showed them *Eraserhead*. So, right then, I could have passed away peaceful and happy.

I like all of Kubrick's films, but my favorite may be *Lolita*. I just like the world. I like the characters. I love the performances. James Mason is phenomenal beyond the beyond in this film.

We are like the spider.

We weave our life and then move along in it.

We are like the dreamer who dreams and then lives in the dream.

This is true for the entire universe.

UPANISHADS

When we began, there wasn't any *INLAND EMPIRE*, there wasn't anything. I just bumped into Laura Dern on the street, discovering that she was my new neighbor. I hadn't seen her for a long time, and she said, "David, we've got to do something together again." And I said, "We sure do. Maybe I'll write something for you. And maybe we'll do it as an experiment for the Internet." And she said, "Fine."

So I wrote a fourteen-page monologue, and Laura memorized all fourteen pages, and it was about a seventy-minute take. And she was so phenomenal. I couldn't release it on the Internet because it was too good, and it drove me crazy, because there was something about this that held a secret for more. And I would ponder over this thing. And something more would emerge. And that would lead to another scene. But I wouldn't know what in the world it was, and it didn't really make much sense. But then, another idea would come for another scene. And maybe this one, the third one, was very far removed from the first two, even though the second was quite a jump from the first.

One day we were getting ready to shoot a scene called "The Little House," which involved Laura Dern and my friend Krzysztof Majchrzak, an actor from Poland. Krzysztof arrived in Los Angeles fresh from Poland and the CamerImage gang brought him over to my house. When he got out of the car, he was wearing these goofy glasses, and he smiled and pointed to the glasses.

So I got the idea that he planned to wear these things in the scene and I said, "No, no, no, Krzysztof." And he said, "I need a prop. I need a thing." So I went into my office and I opened up the cupboard and saw a little piece of broken tile, I saw a rock, and I saw a red lightbulb, but very transparent like a Christmas light. I took these things out and offered him a choice. "Take one of these, Krzysztof"—and he picked up the bulb. I put the other things away. I wasn't going to let him have those any-more. I just gave him the bulb. So we went out to the small house and Krzysztof came out from behind a tree with the red bulb in his mouth, and that's how we shot the scene. So one thing led to another.

I really had this feeling that if there's a Unified Field, there must be a unity be-tween a Christmas tree bulb and this man from Poland who came in wearing these strange glasses. It's interesting to see how these unrelated things live together. And it gets your mind working. How do these things relate when they seem so far apart? It conjures up a third thing that almost unifies those first two. It's a struggle to see how this unity in the midst of diversity could go to work. The ocean is the unity and these things float on it.

And I thought, *Well, obviously, there's got to be a way that these relate—because of this great Unified Field.* There couldn't be a fragment that doesn't relate to everything. It's all kind of one thing, I felt. So, I had high hopes that there would be a unity emerging, that I would see the way these things all related, one to another. But it wasn't until halfway through that, suddenly, I saw a kind of form that would unite the rest, every-thing that had come before. And that was a big day. That was a good day, because I could pretty much say that it would be a feature film.

One day, still very early in the process, I was talking to Laura Dern and learned that her now husband, Ben Harper, is from the Inland Empire in Los Angeles. We were talking along, and she mentioned that. I don't know when it popped up, but I said, "That is the title of this film." I knew nothing about the film at the time. But I wanted to call it *INLAND EMPIRE*.

My parents have a log cabin up in Montana. And my brother, cleaning up there one day, found a scrapbook behind a dresser. He sent it to me, because it was my little scrapbook from when I was five years old, from when I lived in Spokane, Washington. I opened up this scrapbook, and the first picture in it was an aerial view of Spokane. And underneath it said, "Inland Empire." So I figured I was on the right track.

Working on *INLAND EMPIRE* was very different. We shot it entirely in digital video, so the level of flexibility and control was amazing.

Also, I didn't have a script. I wrote the thing scene by scene, without much of a clue where it would end. It was a risk, but I had this feeling that because all things are unified, this idea over here would somehow relate to that idea over there. And I was working with a very great company, StudioCanal in France, who believed in me—enough to let me find my way.

I don't do director's commentary tracks on my DVD releases. I know people enjoy extras, but now, with all the add-ons, the film just seems to have gotten lost. We've got to guard the film itself. It should stand alone. You work so hard to get a film a certain way; it shouldn't be fiddled with. Director's commentaries just open a door to changing people's take on the number one thing—the film. I do believe in telling stories surrounding a film, but to comment as it's rolling is a sacrilege.

Instead, I think you should try to see the whole film through, and try to see it in a quiet place, on as big a screen as you can with as good a sound system as you can. Then you can go into that world and have that experience.

THE DEATH OF FILM

I'm through with film as a medium. For me, film is dead. If you look at what people all over the world are taking still pictures with now, you begin to see what's going to happen.

I'm shooting in digital video and I love it. I have a Web site and I started doing small experiments for the site with these small cameras, at first thinking they were just like little toys, and they were not very good. But then I started realizing that they're very, very good—for me, at least.

You have forty-minute takes, automatic focus. They're lightweight. And you can see what you've shot right away. With film you have to go into the lab and you don't see what you've shot until the next day, but with DV, as soon as you're done, you can put it into the computer and go right to work. And there are so many tools. A thousand tools were born this morning, and there'll be ten thousand new tools tomorrow. It happened first in sound. Now everybody's got ProTools, and you can manipulate these sounds, just fine-tune them unbelievably fast. The same thing's happening with the image. It gives you so much control.

I started thinking and experimenting. I did some tests from DV to film, because you still have to transfer to film to show in the theater. And although it does not look exactly like it was shot on film, it looks way better than I would have thought.

Once you start working in that world of DV with small, lightweight equipment and automatic focus, working with film seems so cumbersome. These 35mm film cameras are starting to look like dinosaurs to me. They're huge; they weigh tons. And you've got to move them around. There are so many things that have to be done, and it's all so slow. It kills a lot of possibilities. With DV everything is lighter; you're more mobile. It's far more fluid. You can think on your feet and catch things.

And for actors, to get down into a character in the middle of a scene and then suddenly have to stop while we reload the film cameras after ten minutes—often, this breaks the thing. But now you're rolling along; you've got forty minutes down in there. And you can start talking to the actors, and instead of stopping it you can move in and push it. You can even rehearse while you're shooting, although I start goofing up the soundtrack, because they've got to chop out all my words. But many times I am talking to the actors while we are shooting and we are able to get in deeper and deeper.

My advice is to use the opportunity DV brings to do what you truly believe in. Keep your own voice. Don't do anything for the sole purpose of impressing any studio or some money people. That always seems to backfire, in my experience. It's great to go to film school, and you can get a lot of intellectual knowledge there, but learn by doing. And now that costs have fallen, you can really go and do it on your own. Then there are lots of film festivals that you can enter and see if you can catch some distribution or financial help later on.

The DV camera I currently use is a Sony PD-150, which is a lower quality than HD. And I *love* this lower quality. I love the small cameras.

The quality reminds me of the films of the 1930s. In the early days, the emulsion wasn't so good, so there was less information on the screen. The Sony PD result is a bit like that; it's nowhere near high-def. And sometimes, in a frame, if there's some question about what you're seeing, or some dark corner, the mind can go dreaming. If everything is crystal clear in that frame, that's what it is—that's *all* it is.

And high-def, unfortunately, is so crystal clear. I saw a piece of film on the screen in my mixing room shot in high-def; it was some kind of science fiction. And in the background, I could see wood screws in what was supposed to be a metal console. It's going to be far more difficult to build sets for high-def.

How we see films is changing. The video iPod and videos online are changing everything. A tiny little picture, instead of a giant big picture, is going to be how people see films. And the good news: At least people will have their headphones. Sound will become, I think, even more important. But then maybe you can put the iPod in something and squirt the image on a big screen in your home, have subwoofers and beautiful speaker systems and quietness in the house, so that you can fall into this world.

The whole thing is, when those curtains open, and the lights go down, we must be able to go into that world. And in many ways, it's getting very difficult to go into a world. People talk so much in theaters. And there's a tiny, crummy little picture. How do you get that experience?

I think it's going to be a bit of a bumpy road. But the possibility is there for very clean pictures—no scratches, no dirt, no water marks, no tearing—and an image that can be controlled in an infinite number of ways. If you take care of how you show a film, it can be a beautiful experience that lets you go into a world. We're still working out ways for that to happen. But digital is here; the video iPod is here; we've just got to get real and roll with the flow.

COMMON SENSE

Most of filmmaking is common sense. If you stay on your toes and think about how to do a thing, it's right there.

ADVICE

Stay true to yourself. Let your voice ring out, and don't let anybody fiddle with it. Never turn down a good idea, but never take a bad idea. And meditate. It's very important to experience that Self, that pure consciousness. It's really helped me. I think it would help any filmmaker. So start diving within, enlivening that bliss consciousness. Grow in happiness and intuition. Experience the joy of doing. And you'll glow in this peaceful way. Your friends will be very, very happy with you. Everyone will want to sit next to you. And people will give you money!

SLEEP

Sleep is really important. You need to rest the physiology to be able to work well and meditate well. When I don't get enough sleep, my meditations are duller. You may even dip into sleep at the beginning of your meditation, because you're settling down. But if you're well rested, you'll have a clearer, deeper experience.

Maybe even in a sleepy meditation you're transcending a little. But it's far better to have a very clear, clean system as you go in. And when you dive, it's very powerful, very deep.

When you meditate, the mind settles down to that deepest level, and the physiology settles down right behind it. And now, through lots of research, they know that in that deepest state in meditation, you're getting three times deeper rest than that of the deepest sleep. Still, sleep is important to prepare you to get to that level.

KEEP AT IT

It's such a tricky business. You want to do your art, but you've got to live. So you've got to have a job, and then sometimes you're too tired to do your art.

But if you love what you're doing, you're going to keep on doing it anyway. I've been very lucky. Along the way, there are people who help us. I've had plenty of those people in my life who've helped me go to the next step. And you get that help because you've done something, so you have to keep doing it.

So much of what happened to me is good fortune. But I would say: Try to get a job that gives you some time; get your sleep and a little bit of food; and work as much as you can. There's so much enjoyment in doing what you love. Maybe this will open doors, and you'll find a way to do what you love. I hope you do.

In some ways, the more films you've done, the easier it is to make one. You become familiar with the process of catching an idea and translating that idea. You understand the tools and the lighting. You understand the whole process—you've been through it before.

But it's also harder, because when you release another film, it's seen in context of what you've already done. It's going to be judged based on that. And if you've just come off something successful, you feel that you may take the fall.

But if you've come down from something very low, as I did after *Dune*, there may be zero fear—you feel you can't get any lower. You may experience this euphoria and freedom that you have nothing to lose.

You have to learn to find balance in success and failure. Success can kill you just as failure can. And the only way to have balance in success and failure is to function on that Unified Field level. There's your friend. You can't fake it—you're either in that field or you're not. And when that field is fully enlivened, you can't lose, no matter what happens.

Curving back upon My own Nature,

I create again and again.

BHAGAVAD-GITA

When you finish a project, there's a good feeling to it, but there's something of a vacuum, too. You've been putting all your attention on that, and then it's done.

It's like fishing. You caught a beautiful fish yesterday, and you're out today with the same bait, and you're wondering if you're going to catch another. But if you carry on the analogy of fishing, sometimes, even if you sit with lots and lots of patience, no fish come. You're in the wrong area. And so maybe you reel in the hook, get the paddle, and move to another place. That means you leave the chair where you're daydreaming or you move on to another thing. Just by changing something, the desire often gets fulfilled.

It doesn't mean that if you just sit and wait that it will come. I don't know quite what brings it. But the desire, if it's kept alive, will often be validated with an idea. When you get an idea, you know you've got a validation.

COMPASSION

Softer than the flower where kindness is concerned,
Stronger than the thunder where principles are at stake.

VEDIC DESCRIPTION OF THE ENLIGHTENED

Meditation is not a selfish thing. Even though you're diving in and experiencing the Self, you're not closing yourself off from the world. You're strengthening yourself, so that you can be more effective when you go back out into the world.

It's like they say on airplanes: "First put your mask on, and then help those next to you put theirs on." My friend Charlie Lutes used to say, "There's a guy crying on the curb, and you sit down to comfort him, and pretty soon there's *two* guys crying on the curb."

So compassion, appreciation for others, and the capacity to help others are enhanced when you meditate. You start diving down and experiencing this ocean of pure love, pure peace—you could say pure compassion. You experience that, and know it by being it. *Then* you go out into the world, and you can really do something for people.

One of the main things that got me talking publicly about Transcendental Meditation was seeing the difference it can make to kids. Kids are suffering. Stress is now hitting them at a younger and younger age, at just about the time they get out of the crib. And there are all these different learning disorders that I never even heard about before.

At the same time, I saw the results of consciousness-based education, which is education that develops the full potential of the human being. It's the same education everyone receives, with the added bonus that the student learns to dive within and unfold that Self, that pure consciousness.

There's a school principal, Dr. George Rutherford, in Washington, D.C., who has introduced Transcendental Meditation into three schools. Before that, the schools were filled with violence: There were shootings, suicides, and violence. But he got the staff meditating, got the teachers meditating, got the students meditating, and watched it all turn around.

There's another principal, Carmen N'Namdi, in Detroit, who introduced Transcendental Meditation in her school, Nataki Talibah, about nine years ago. The kids meditate ten minutes in the morning together, ten minutes in the afternoon, and the school is a blissful school. Those kids are happier, getting better grades, and going out and experiencing all kinds of success.

It's something that works. You take in more intellectual knowledge during school because it's so much fun. But you're also expanding the container of that knowledge. You contrast that with what normal education produces, which is a joke. It's facts and figures, but the knower does not know him- or herself.

One night I saw a play at Maharishi School in Iowa—a school that has consciousness-based education. It was a cold and rainy night, and when I was told I was going to see a high school play, I thought, "Man, it's going to be a very long night." I was sitting in the middle of this little theater, a beautiful little theater, and out on stage came the students. They weren't professional actors; they were just kids putting on a play. But I was never more blown away. I thought it was better than a Broadway production, because what I saw was consciousness on these faces—a lively, glowing consciousness.

They had such intelligence and timing, and their humor was right on the money. You don't worry about students like that. They're self-sufficient. They're going to do fine in the world and they're going to make the world better by being in it.

My foundation, the David Lynch Foundation for Consciousness-Based Education and World Peace, was set up to help more kids get that kind of experience. We've raised money and given it to schools all over the country for thousands and thousands of students to learn to meditate. And it's amazing to see kids who do this. Stress just doesn't catch them; it's like water off a duck's back.

I want to do this not only for those students' sake, for their own growth of consciousness, but for all of us, because we are like lightbulbs. And, like lightbulbs, we can enjoy that brighter light of consciousness within, and also radiate it. I believe that the key to peace is in this.

If there were ten thousand new meditating students, it would affect this country. It would be like a wave of peace. It's harmony, coherence—real peace. In the individual, that light of consciousness drives negativity further and further away. In the world, it can do the same thing.

REAL PEACE

Avert the danger

that has not yet come.

YOGA SUTRAS

People are so convinced we can't have peace that it's a joke now. Somebody wins a beauty pageant, and the joke is, she wants world peace. And everybody has a big laugh. Nobody believes in peace. It's a nice idea. But that's all it is—just a sweet-little-old-lady idea. It's meaningless. It's never going to happen. And we live in this hellhole, and we think it's got to be this way.

But what if we're wrong?

We know that in one human being, when you ramp up consciousness—when you ramp up that light of unity—negative things begin to recede. In that individual, you see more and more intelligence, more and more creativity, more and more bliss, negativity going away, and a positive influence pouring out into the world. So if there were many, many meditators, it would be beautiful. But even without that, small groups of advanced meditators could still make a huge difference.

The theory is that if the square root of 1 percent of the world's population, or 8,000 people, practices advanced meditation techniques in a group, then that group, according to published research, is quadratically more powerful than the same number scattered about.

These peace-creating groups have been formed for short-term studies. And every time the advanced meditators got together in a group, they dramatically affected the area around them. They measurably reduced crime and violence. How did they do that?

There is a field of unity within everyone. It's always been there. It's unbounded, infinite, and eternal. It's that level of life that never had a beginning. It is, and it will be, forever. And it can be enlivened. In the human being, the enlivening of that field leads to enlightenment—the full potential of the individual. In the world, the result of enlivening unity by a peace-creating group would be real peace on earth.

I'd like to say: I deeply love film; I love catching ideas; and I love to meditate. I love enlivening unity. And I think the enlivening of unity brings a better and better life. Maybe enlightenment is far away, but it's said that when you walk toward the light, with every step, things get brighter. Every day, for me, gets better and better. And I believe that enlivening unity in the world will bring peace on earth. So I say: Peace to all of you.

May everyone be happy. May everyone be free of disease.
May auspiciousness be seen everywhere. May suffering belong to no one.
Peace.

Right now I'm catching some painting fish. And some music fish. I haven't caught the next film fish yet. I just try to catch ideas—and sometimes I fall in love with one and then I know what I want to do. It has nothing to do with money; just with translating that idea.

After *INLAND EMPIRE*, people asked me whether I would distribute a film again myself. And, with a team, I would for sure. Likewise, I remain completely committed to shooting in digital video. DV is just like film, without the problems. We live in a digital world now, and I love it—I'm never going back to film. So far as the reaction to *INLAND EMPIRE*, it went, I think, like it does for a lot of films: It was hated by some and loved by some. And it made a discussion. The blogs were lively.

I do believe film students themselves are going digital. Of course, film students will always experience a yearning to make at least one film using film, just to have done it, just to have been in that world. But after doing that, I think, they will quickly return to the digital world.

Looking ahead, I am commited to my work with the Foundation. We want to help the rapidly growing number of schools that are asking for programs in meditation. And the word is going around that diving within really changes things for the good. It is not something that just comes and goes—when you give students this technique, things really start changing. And they have that technique for the rest of their lives. I see that people are coming to realize that it is just so beautiful: this dive within, this transcending, and this experience of the Unified Field, where everything comes from. It is a Field of pure bliss consciousness, absolute intelligence, and infinite creativity.

Everything I experience today brings me back again and again to where I started: True happiness lies within.

DAVID LYNCH'S INTERVIEWS
WITH PAUL MCCARTNEY
AND RINGO STARR

On April 4, 2009, Paul McCartney and Ringo Starr, among other artists, performed a benefit concert at Radio City Music Hall in New York City for the David Lynch Foundation for Consciousness-Based Education and World Peace. Following rehearsals the day before the benefit, David Lynch conducted separate interviews with Paul and Ringo about their experiences with Transcendental Meditation and creativity. They appear here for the first time in print.

DAVID LYNCH'S INTERVIEW
WITH PAUL MCCARTNEY

David Lynch: When did you first hear about Transcendental Meditation and what did you make of it?

Paul McCartney: It was actually George Harrison's wife, Pattie, who had heard that Maharishi was coming to town. And she said, "We should all go." At that time I was personally not in a good place. I was overdoing it in the sixties. I was not very centered and I was looking for something; I think we all were. We heard that Maharishi was going to give a lecture in a London hotel. That was the first time I heard about meditation. But we'd actually seen Maharishi when we were kids growing up in Liverpool, because, as you know, he had traveled around the world seven times to spread his message of Transcendental Meditation. We remembered he seemed so happy, and we just thought, "He's so cool!"

David: What did you think of Maharishi's message?

Paul: It was very interesting, it was very calming, and it seemed like something that was worth trying. He put it very well, he made it seem simple, he made it seem very attractive, and so I think we were all just sold. Maharishi's personality had a lot to do with it. He had a very infectious sense of humor, so I think that was very appealing as well. It was a great message; it was something I think we felt we needed, but he also put it over in this way that was very attractive.

David: Did Maharishi personally teach you?

Paul: Yes. We went to Bangor, in Wales, where we attended a seminar with Maharishi and he gave us each a mantra, which, looking back, it was definitely a great occasion. It was terrific. He often used to carry flowers, so there was this feeling of connection with nature that was very grounding. One by one we went into a room where Maharishi was and he just talked very quietly for a little while and then he said, "I'm going to say your mantra, and I want you to repeat it to me once to make sure you've got it, and then I don't want you to ever say it again. You don't need to verbalize it. You want to keep it inside." And so he did. He just leaned over and he whispered my mantra and I heard it clearly. I whispered it back and he said, "Yes." And he smiled. And so that was it, really.

David: Then you had your first meditation?

Paul: And then we each went and meditated the way that Maharishi taught us. And over the next few days, we would report back from time to time, and then eventually we all went to Rishikesh in India with Maharishi, which was a more sustained time with him.

David: What was the experience like in Rishikesh?

Paul: It was great. There was nothing fancy about it. We would wake up, go for a light breakfast, socialize a bit with the other people who were on the course, and then go back to our rooms for our morning meditation. Each of us had little rooms, which were very simple, but adequate. We would sit and meditate. And then there was lunch, and again we'd socialize and chat, and then we'd meditate in the afternoons. Sometimes Maharishi would have a meeting where we could talk to him about our experiences and he would guide us. And then in the evening, there was a question-and-answer session in a hall with Maharishi.

David: Did you enjoy your experience there?

Paul: I enjoyed the whole experience. There were some very blissful moments in meditation. I remember one in particular when I'd been meditating for a while and I got to a really good place, and I remember the feeling was that I was like a feather floating over a hot air pipe. It was a very nice feeling and I remember that vividly and I reported that to Maharishi and he laughed, "Yes, this is good. Such a joy."

David: How many songs did you write in Rishikesh?

Paul: We wrote quite a few songs between us. It was inspirational being there. During the times when we weren't meditating, we had our guitars and we'd do quite a bit of writing. We just felt good. I'd be meditating and I'd start thinking about a song and then I'd think, "Go away, thoughts. I'll deal with you later. Go away." And I would come back to my mantra. But thoughts were okay. We talked to Maharishi about it; he said, "This is fine. You know, this is what happens."

David: After Rishikesh, did you see Maharishi again?

Paul: I saw him much later, after my wife, Linda, passed away. I went with two of my children to see him where he was in Holland. It was lovely to see him again—he was such a great presence to be in.

David: What are your thoughts about what is happening with Transcendental Meditation today?

Paul: It's fabulous how the David Lynch Foundation is putting the meditation in schools. It's great to talk about meditation, but when you actually put it in the mainstream, I think that's very important because then people can say, "Ah, in

Detroit, where the David Lynch Foundation has put the program into schools, here are the results." This is what people need. They don't need high-minded talk so much as results. So to be able to say, "The kids in Detroit love it. The kids in the West Bank love it. The kids in Brazil love it." And the fact that you're actually getting results—that's what's important. It's like if you have a great acorn seed but if you don't put it in the ground, it's pretty guaranteed you won't get an oak tree. But if you put it in the ground, there's a very good chance you'll get an oak tree. And that's what is happening today. And that's why Ringo and I were so happy to do the concert. And why everyone who's doing the show is here for the same reason. It's very inspiring.

David Lynch: Where were you when you first heard about Transcendental Meditation?

Ringo Starr: I was in England, and my first wife and I, we were having our second son. I came back from the hospital that night and there were messages from George and John. They'd been to the Hilton Hotel to hear Maharishi speak and they said, "We've met this man, Maharishi, and we're all going to Wales in a couple of weeks. You've got to come!" So I went to Wales to be with Maharishi at a college. But then, as you know, a sad thing happened; while we were there Brian Epstein died. So we didn't stay too long; we all came back to London. That was my first introduction. Maharishi was so cool because he didn't know who the hell we were. But when we got off the train he saw all these fans—you know that was 1967, and it was Beatle madness!

Suddenly, Maharishi had this great idea. "Oh, you can go on a world tour and we could open a meditation center everywhere we stop!" Then a few months later we all went to Rishikesh, in India, to Maharishi's ashram. It was an incredible journey, but I was only there two weeks because our baby wasn't that old. We gave ourselves two weeks to experience everything that was going on. There were several other musicians there too, like Donovan, et cetera.

It was interesting because Maharishi was always smiling. I really wanted the joy that Maharishi had. That's what I saw, a great joy. And so he gave us all a mantra, and we would all meditate together. I remember we had this one group meditation on the rooftop of one of the halls, and the energy was so powerful.

For me, meditation gives me a moment to stop the thinking and let my heart come forward. That's how I've always felt about it, because my thinking will drive me barmy!

David: Do you remember the time when Maharishi first taught you to meditate?

Ringo: Yes, very clearly. Maharishi gave me my mantra, and I made a promise not to tell anyone else my mantra. The meditation gave me a moment to be quiet. I have such good thoughts about Maharishi.

David: How do you think Transcendental Meditation serves creativity?

Ringo: It gives you a break from the madness—I can't put it any other way, really.

David: What was your earliest memory of music?

Ringo: I came from Liverpool and I was quite ill when I was young. I was thirteen or fourteen years old and I had tuberculosis. There was a lot of tuberculosis in the 1950s. They sent me to a hospital in the country that was surrounded by fields. And to keep us busy, once every three or four weeks, a music teacher would come in with all these percussion instruments, including a drum, a tambourine, a maraca, a triangle, and a big sheet with green dots, red dots, and blue dots. If the teacher pointed to the red dot you'd hit the drum and if he pointed at the yellow you'd shake the tambourine. Anyway, I played drum the very first week, and after that I wouldn't play in the band unless I got to play the drums. That's how drumming came into my life! So, I got out of the hospital and went home and made my first kit out of biscuit tins. The years went on and I still couldn't afford drums, but I would look at them in windows. One day, my stepfather went to London because one of his relations had died. The man had been a drummer. My stepfather bought his drum kit for, like, twenty dollars and brought it back to me.

It was a great drum kit but, you know, I was seventeen or eighteen, and I wanted a new kit. So I sold it and went to a music store and bought an Ajax drum kit, which just looked great! Of course, I didn't know how to play it, but that's how it started. I just never wanted to play anything else. My grandparents even had a piano, but I had no interest. Same with guitars . . . I just felt, "I'm a drummer—that's what I do."

David: When did you first meet the other Beatles?

Ringo: In Germany. I was playing with Rory Storm and the Hurricanes, and we played in some of the same clubs. And then I came back to England and I would go see them play. They were the only band I really went to see because I loved the front line with John, Paul, and George. And then one day, I was home and there was a knock on the door and it was Brian Epstein saying, "Would you come and play a lunchtime session with the Beatles?" I said, "Sure," and that's how it started. I was still playing with Rory and the Hurricanes, but I would occasionally play with the Beatles. One time, I was playing at a holiday camp in England and Brian called and said, "Would you join the band?" I said, "Yes," and as they say, the rest is history. But people forget that we were a cover band in those early days. John and Paul weren't writing all those songs right away. But then their writing came into force. I feel that John and Paul are the two finest voices, and Paul is still the most incredible bass player.

David: Here's my Beatle story: When the Beatles first arrived in the United States, everybody remembers they went to New York City, but they didn't play there first; they went down to Washington, D.C., and I was at their concert that night, but I couldn't hear them. I was pretty close and I still could hardly hear their voices—it was wall-to-wall screams. When the concert was over, the police made a barricade on both sides of the stairway for the Beatles to leave. I saw a man leap over the police and pull out a tuft of hair from one of the Beatles!

Ringo: Well, it wasn't me that day, thank you, Lord!

David: I had gone to the concert because my girlfriend was in love with the Beatles. I wanted to see what it was all about—plus, I loved their music.

Ringo: Who was her favorite?

David: Ringo!

Eraserhead (1977)

The Elephant Man (1980)

Blue Velvet (1986)

Wild at Heart (1990)

Twin Peaks (1990–1991, 2017)

Lost Highway (1997)

The Straight Story (1999)

Mulholland Drive (2001)

INLAND EMPIRE (2006)

SOURCES QUOTED

Ramayana. Retold by William Buck. University of California Press, 1976.

Eternal Stories from the Upanishads. Thomas Egenes and Kumuda Reddy. Smriti Books, 2002.

Maharishi Mahesh Yogi on the Bhagavad-Gita: A New Translation and Commentary, Chapters 1–6. International SRM Publications, 1967. Penguin Books, 1969.

Maharishi's Absolute Theory of Defence. Maharishi Mahesh Yogi. Age of Enlightenment Publications, 1996.

The Upanishads. Translated by Alistair Shearer and Peter Russell. Harper & Row, 1978.

Three-time Oscar-nominated director David Lynch is among the leading filmmakers of our era. From the early seventies to the present day, Lynch's popular and critically acclaimed film projects, which include *Eraserhead*, *The Elephant Man*, *Wild at Heart*, *Blue Velvet*, *Mulholland Drive*, *INLAND EMPIRE*, and *Twin Peaks*, are internationally considered to have broken down the wall between art-house cinema and Hollywood moviemaking.

You can visit the David Lynch Foundation for Consciousness-Based Education and World Peace at www.DavidLynchFoundation.org. The author's proceeds from the sale of this book go to the foundation for the purpose of providing funding for in-school programs in Transcendental Meditation.